BIBLE STORY
Dot-to-Dots
COLORING BOOK

Illustrated by Judith Pfeiffer

The purchase of this coloring book grants you the rights
to photocopy the contents for classroom use.

Notice: It is unlawful to copy these pages for resale purposes.
Copy permission is for private use only.

Warner
Press Kids™
educate • nurture • inspire
www.warnerpress.org

305800211014

What did God make at the beginning of time?
Connect the dots.

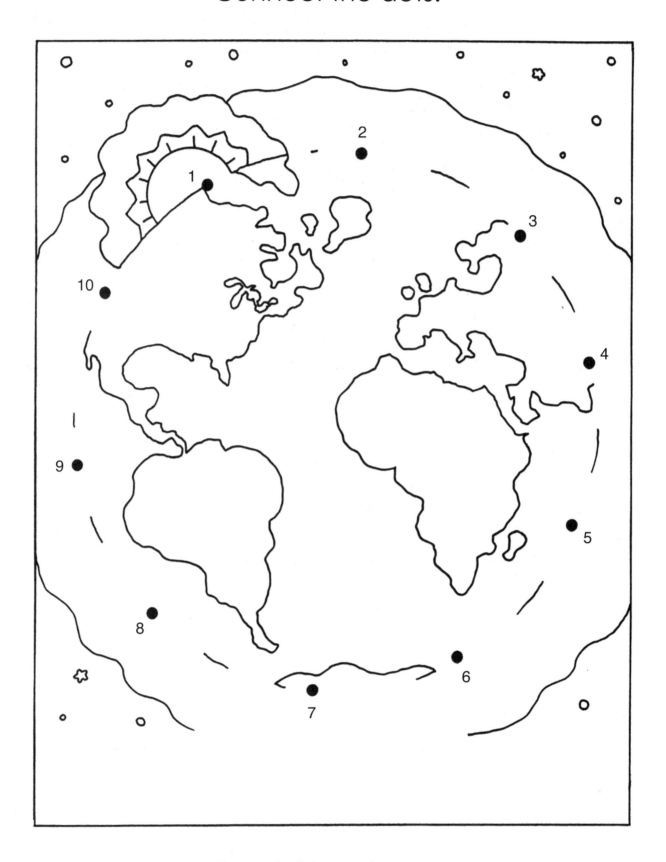

Read Genesis 1:1.

What did Noah see in the sky when God promised never to send a flood over the whole earth again? Connect the dots.

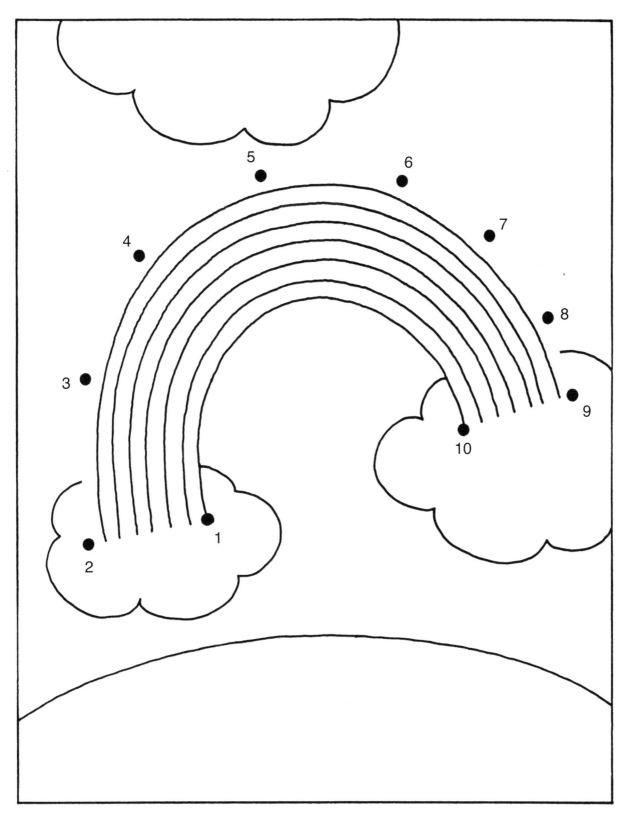

Read Genesis 9:14-15.

What did the people try to build to reach the heavens? Connect the dots.

Read Genesis 11:4.

What did Moses see one time when God wanted to talk to him? Connect the dots.

Read Exodus 3:1-4.

What did God write the 10 Commandments on?
Connect the dots.

Read Exodus 32:18.

What instrument did the priests play as they marched around the walls of Jericho? Connect the dots.

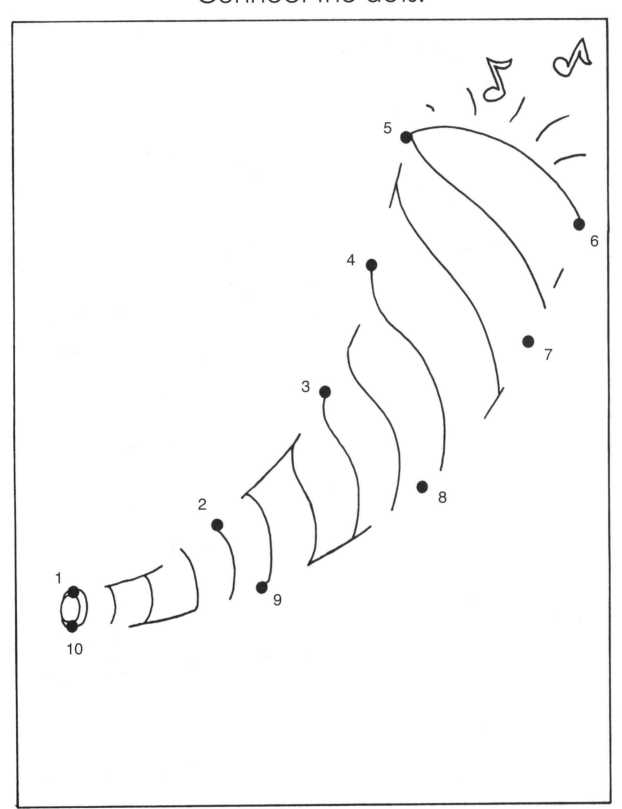

Read Joshua 6:8.

What did David use to kill a giant?
Connect the dots.

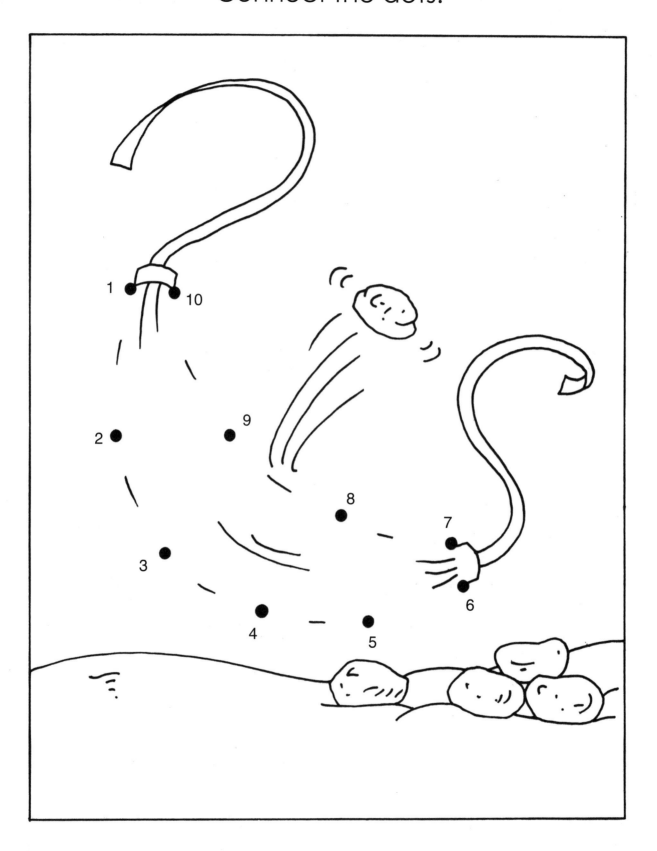

Read 1 Samuel 17:40.

What swallowed Jonah because he disobeyed God? Connect the dots.

Read Jonah 1:17.

What did the Wise Men see when they were looking for Jesus?
Connect the dots.

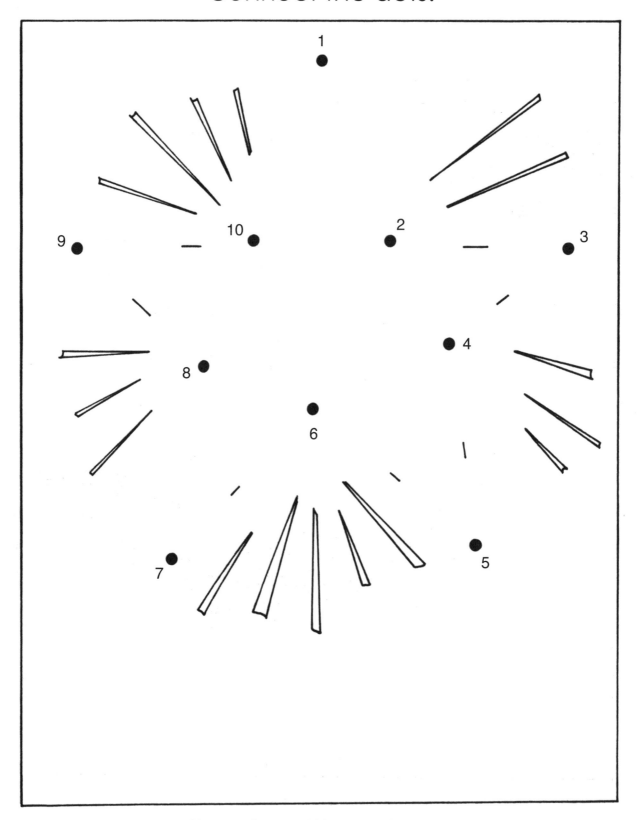

Read Matthew 2:1-2.

What were Simon and Andrew doing when Jesus asked them to follow Him? Connect the dots.

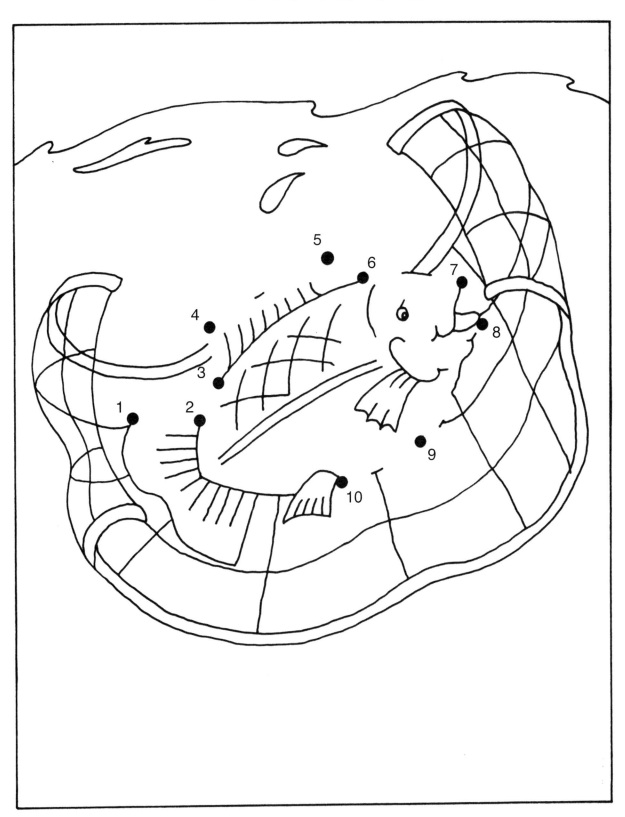

Read Mark 1:16-18.

What did God's Spirit look like when it came down from heaven after Jesus was baptized? Connect the dots.

Read Matthew 3:16.

What did the Good Samaritan use to take the hurt man to the inn?
Connect the dots.

Read Luke 10:34.

When his money was gone, what was the Prodigal Son's job? Connect the dots.

Read Luke 15:14-16.

Jesus loved us so much He died to save us from our sins. What did soldiers nail Jesus to? Connect the dots.

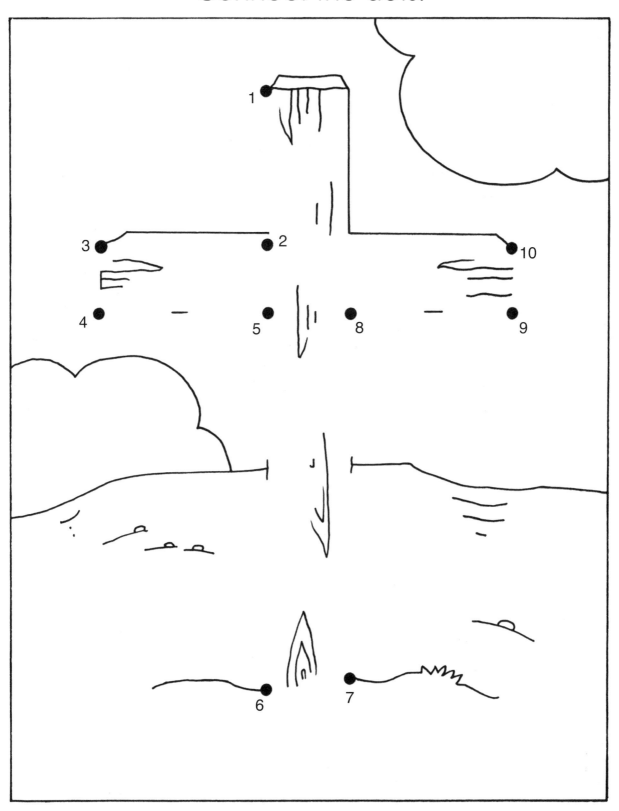

Read John 19:16-18.

What creature bit Paul when he was putting wood on the fire? Connect the dots.

Read Acts 28:1-3.